Canadian Mounties

by Sabrina Crewe

CAPSTONE PRESS
a capstone imprint

Pebble Plus is published by Capstone Press,
1710 Roe Crest Drive, North Mankato, Minnesota 56003
www.capstonepub.com

Library of Congress Cataloging-in-Publication Data
Cataloging-in-publication information is on file with the Library of Congress.

ISBN 978–1-4914-7094-7 (library binding : alk. paper)
ISBN 978–1-4914-7100-5 (pbk. : alk. paper)
ISBN 978–1-4914-7112-8 (eBook PDF)

Developed and Produced by Discovery Books Limited
Paul Humphrey: project manager
Sabrina Crewe: editor
Ian Winton: designer

Photo Credits
Mariemily Photos/Shutterstock: cover; RCMP-GRC © (2002–2014) Her Majesty the Queen in Right of Canada as represented by the Royal Canadian Mounted Police: title page, 7 (bottom), 9 (both), 11 (inset), 13 (both), 15 (both), 17, 19, 21; Tyler McKay/Shutterstock: 5; Pete Spiro/Shutterstock: 7 (top); Paul McKinnon/Shutterstock: 11 (main image).

Note to Parents and Teachers

This book describes and illustrates Canadian Mounties. The images support early readers in understanding text. The repetition of words and phrases helps early readers learn new words. This book also introduces early readers to subject-specific vocabulary words, which are defined in the Glossary section. Early readers may need assistance to read some words and to use the Table of Contents, Glossary, Read More, Internet Sites, and Index sections of the book.

Printed in China through World Print Ltd in 2014
007272WPS15

Table of Contents

A Symbol for Canada

A Mountie on horseback is
a famous symbol of Canada.
A symbol is a picture or thing
that stands for something
important. Symbols can
stand for ideas, beliefs,
and countries.

"Mountie" is short for Mounted Police. The word *mounted* means riding on a horse.

Becoming a Mountie

The Mounties began in 1873. The first Mounties went to western parts of Canada. They were called the North-West Mounted Police. In 1920, they became the Royal Canadian Mounted Police.

This postage stamp celebrated Mounties about 80 years ago.

These Mounties lived in Saskatchewan more than 100 years ago.

Mounties train for six months to become police officers. They can start work when they are 19 years old. Mounties must speak French or English. They should be fit and healthy.

Mounties learn to be strong and fast.

Mounties wear uniforms to show that they are police officers. The Mounties' famous red jackets are for special occasions. They wear other uniforms for their everyday work.

What Mounties Do

Mounties do all kinds of police work. They arrest people who break the law. They protect people who are in danger. People often say, "Mounties always get their man!"

Mounties protect children.

These Mounties are on patrol in a police car.

The Mounties have their own
Air Services. Their aircraft
patrol Canada from the sky.
Mounties use boats, too.
They watch over Canada's
coasts, rivers, and lakes.

A police helicopter

A Mountie patrol on water

15

Mounties have more than 100 dog teams across Canada. The dogs start to train when they are one year old. Mountie dogs track and rescue lost people. They help find clues to crimes.

A Mountie dog and
dog handler

Mounties in the Community

Mounties have a special show called the Musical Ride. The Musical Ride is like a dance on horseback! Mounties perform Musical Rides in communities around the country.

The riders and horses show their skills in the Musical Ride.

Mounties work hard in communities. They teach children how to be safe. Children everywhere know the Mounties' mascot, Safety Bear. This cuddly bear is the Mounties' own symbol!

Safety Bear visits communities all over Canada.

Glossary

ceremonial—something used for a special occasion

community—a group of people living in the same neighbourhood or area

mascot—something, often an animal, that people use as a good luck symbol

patrol—to go around a place to guard it and stop any crimes from happening

symbol—something that stands for something else. People use symbols to show what is important to them.

train—to learn or get ready for something

uniform—the special outfit that shows a person belongs to a group or team

Read More

Horvath, Polly. *M Is for Mountie: A Royal Canadian Mounted Police Alphabet*. Ann Arbor, MI: Sleeping Bear Press, 2009.

Bellefontaine, Kim and **Per-Henrik Gürth**. *ABC of Canada*. Toronto, ON: Kids Can Press, 2004.

Internet Sites

FactHound offers a safe, fun way to find Internet sites related to this book. All of the sites on FactHound have been researched by our staff.

Here's all you do:

Visit *www.facthound.com*

Type in this code: 9781491470947

 Check out projects, games and lots more at **www.capstonekids.com**

Index

Word Count: 259
Grade: 1
Early-Intervention Level: 17